NATIONAL
GEOGRAPHIC

Ladders

Yellowstone

National Park

Read to find out how and why Yellowstone National Park was created.

Welcome to
YELLOWSTONE
National Park

by Christopher Siegel

Yellowstone is proof of how violent Earth can be. About 640,000 years ago, there was a huge volcanic eruption in the center of what is now Yellowstone National Park. Fast-moving lava flows covered the area. A gigantic crater called a **caldera** remained. Volcanic activity continues in Yellowstone today. Tourists come to see the waterfalls, hot springs, and geysers.

Yellowstone is a beautiful place. The park is located on a high **plateau**. It is a broad, flat area surrounded by mountains. Yellowstone has jagged peaks, lakes, deep canyons, and forests.

Morning Glory Pool is a colorful hot spring. Its water is heated by melted rocks that lie deep underground.

The History of Yellowstone

Yellowstone was established as America's first national park on March 1, 1872, when President Ulysses S. Grant signed the Act of Dedication Law. According to the dedication, the park was to be a wilderness area created "for the benefit and enjoyment of the people."

Yellowstone is the largest park in the lower 48 states, or **continental United States**. Its boundaries are located in three states: Wyoming, Montana, and Idaho. The park is larger than the states of Delaware and Rhode Island combined. Today, the park is part of a larger area called the Greater Yellowstone Ecosystem. An **ecosystem** is made up of all the plants, animals, and nonliving things in an environment. Each part of the ecosystem affects all the other parts.

1700s The human history of the park begins at least 11,000 years ago when people use the area as their home and as hunting and fishing grounds. Native American groups continue to live in the area. In the late 1700s, the first people of European descent begin exploring the region.

1859 Mountain man Jim Bridger explores the Yellowstone region. As with Colter, few people believe his wild stories.

1700

1800

1808 John Colter is one of the first persons of European descent to explore the Yellowstone region. His stories of "hidden fires, smoking pits, and the smell of brimstone" spark further exploration.

The Hayden Expedition

1872 President Ulysses S. Grant signs a bill into law creating Yellowstone National Park.

1995 The U.S. Fish and Wildlife Service brings wolves back into the area. The wolves thrive. Many wolves live in the Greater Yellowstone Ecosystem today.

1900

2000

1871 The Hayden Expedition is pictured on the previous page. This team of 34 men sets out in seven wagons to survey the Yellowstone region for the U.S. Congress. The survey helps name Yellowstone as America's first national park.

2010 Yellowstone draws nearly 3.6 million tourists. This beats the 2009 record of 3.3 million tourists. Visitors travel to the park to see hot springs, geysers, and wildlife.

5

Facts About Yellowstone

Yellowstone has some of the most interesting natural environments in the world. About 80 percent of the park is forest, and about 15 percent is grassland. The remaining 5 percent is covered by water. More than 67 species of mammals live in Yellowstone. Many animals migrate, or move between environments, within the Greater Yellowstone Ecosystem. These animals are a major park attraction.

Many people visit Yellowstone to see the American bison. In the early 1800s, there were about 50 million bison in North America. But by 1902, there were only about 1,000. Bison living in Yellowstone had large areas to roam, so their herds began to grow. This saved the American bison from becoming extinct.

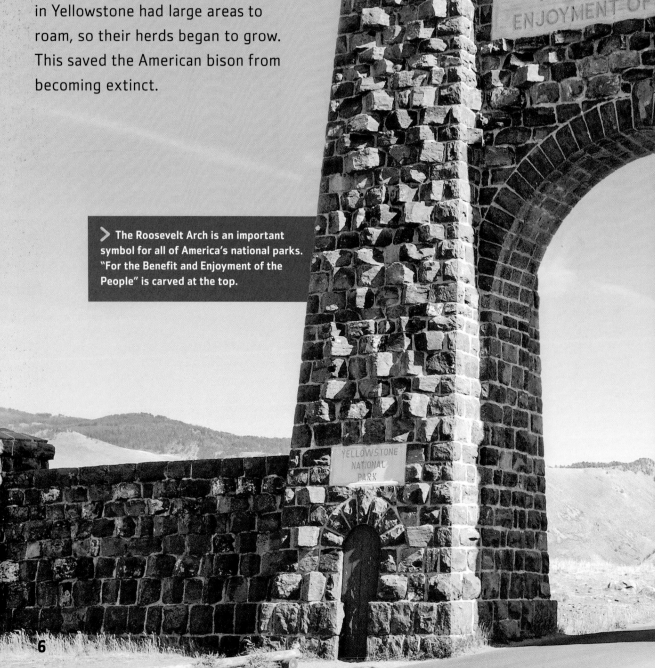

> The Roosevelt Arch is an important symbol for all of America's national parks. "For the Benefit and Enjoyment of the People" is carved at the top.

AND
EOPLE"

CREATED BY
ACT OF CONGRESS
MARCH 1, 1872

∧ The Yellowstone River is the longest undammed river in the continental United States. Its name comes from the yellow sandstone cliffs on either side of it.

∧ Yellowstone contains about one-half of the world's hydrothermal features. There are about 10,000 in the park, including more than 300 geysers.

∧ Bison are the largest land mammals in North America. More than 3,000 bison roam the grasslands of Yellowstone year-round.

Check In Why do you think it is important to preserve the natural environment of Yellowstone?

A Tour of Volcanic
YELLOWSTONE

by Richard Easby

Welcome to Yellowstone National Park! Our tour begins at the north entrance. You can see a land covered in trees, grasses, sparkling lakes, and rushing rivers. Most people come to see Yellowstone's famous wildlife. Look out for bison, grizzly bears, elk, and gray wolves. Besides the 2.2 million acres of wilderness, Yellowstone is also a **geological** wonder. In the past two million years, there have been three major volcanic eruptions. These eruptions helped create the land you see today.

Yellowstone sits on top of a geological hot spot. One of the world's largest volcanoes lies deep under the ground below the park. There is a chamber, or huge, closed-in area, inside the volcano. It is filled with **magma**, or melted rock. The volcano last erupted about 640,000 years ago. Explosions caused part of the magma chamber to collapse, forming a huge crater called a caldera. There are signs of volcanic activity all over the region. Let's find some examples of volcanic activity in Yellowstone!

West Entrance

IDAHO MONTANA WYOMING

Grand Prismatic Spring >

North Entrance

Mammoth
ot Springs

SCENIC VIEW 1

Roosevelt
Arch

MONTANA
WYOMING

Northeast Entrance

Gardner River

SCENIC VIEW 2 Obsidian
Cliff

SCENIC VIEW 6 Petrified
Tree

Yellowstone River

Lamar River

SCENIC VIEW 5 Sizzling Basin
Mud Pots

SCENIC VIEW 3 Grand Prismatic
Spring

Turbid
Lake

SCENIC VIEW 4 Old Faithful
Geyser

Stevenson
Island

East Entrance

Dot
Island

WEST
THUMB

Delusion
Lake

Frank
Island

Yellowstone
Lake

of Tour
ay
oundary
Border

Shoshone
Lake

Flat Mountain Arm

SOUTH
ARM

SOUTHEAST ARM

10 Miles

10 Kilometers

Lewis
Lake

Heart
Lake

Yellowstone River

Snake River

South Entrance

MAMMOTH HOT SPRINGS ↘

Now let's take a tour of Yellowstone. Remember to go back to the map as your guide. Our first stop is Mammoth Hot Springs. These flat, colorful rock formations are called **terraces**. Water, heat, and minerals helped create the step-like terraces. Hot spring water contains calcium carbonate. This mineral bubbles to the surface in more than 50 hot springs at Mammoth. Then it settles on the ground.

Over time, the calcium builds up, forming the terraces you see here. But Earth's surface can change quickly. Minerals can build up in the underground passages through which the water flows, stopping springs in an instant. Dry springs can suddenly begin to flow again. These changes can affect the way the terraces look. Some of the terraces may look very different the next time you visit.

OBSIDIAN CLIFF ↘

SCENIC VIEW 2 Can you imagine a mountain made of glass? Our next stop is Obsidian Cliff. Obsidian is a volcanic rock that looks dark and glassy. The cliff is one of the largest deposits of obsidian in the world. It formed long ago after a volcanic eruption. Hot lava flowed over the land and quickly hardened into this cliff. Obsidian breaks into round, flat pieces with sharp edges, so Native Americans made tools from the obsidian they found here. The obsidian was highly prized, and local people traded obsidian with neighboring groups. Obsidian tools from these cliffs have been found hundreds of miles away.

Obsidian arrowhead

GRAND PRISMATIC SPRING ↘

SCENIC VIEW 3 Our next stop is Grand Prismatic Spring. This colorful hot spring is the largest of its kind in Yellowstone. It is pale blue with a deep blue center. You can also see red, yellow, orange, and green. Algae and bacteria, small living things growing in the hot water, make these colors. Grand Prismatic Spring looks inviting, but don't jump in! The water is hot enough to burn your skin. Plus, the colorful algae are delicate and can take many years to recover. Grand Prismatic Spring gushes about 500 gallons of hot water per minute. Wait until the sun shines through the steam clouds that form above the spring. You may see a rainbow!

OLD FAITHFUL ↗

SCENIC VIEW 4 Next up are nature's water fountains, better known as geysers. There are more than 300 geysers in the park. That's about two-thirds of all geysers on Earth! Yellowstone's most famous geyser is Old Faithful, the geyser we are visiting today. Do you hear that hissing sound becoming louder and louder? Get your camera ready. A tower of scalding water is about to shoot out of the geyser. Each eruption lasts just a few minutes. But in about 90 minutes, Old Faithful will erupt again.

SIZZLING BASIN

SCENIC VIEW 5 To get to our next stop, we will drive along the shore of Yellowstone Lake. Then we will follow the Yellowstone River toward Sizzling Basin. Here, the springs have names such as Black Dragon's Caldron, Sour Lake, and Dragon's Mouth. These springs are not as beautiful as those we saw earlier. They have dark-gray or dark-brown colored water that bubbles, sloshes, and boils. The dark water comes from chemicals found in the rocks. What's that smell? The air smells like sulfur, the smell of rotten eggs! The smell comes from gases mixed with the bubbling water, and bacteria.

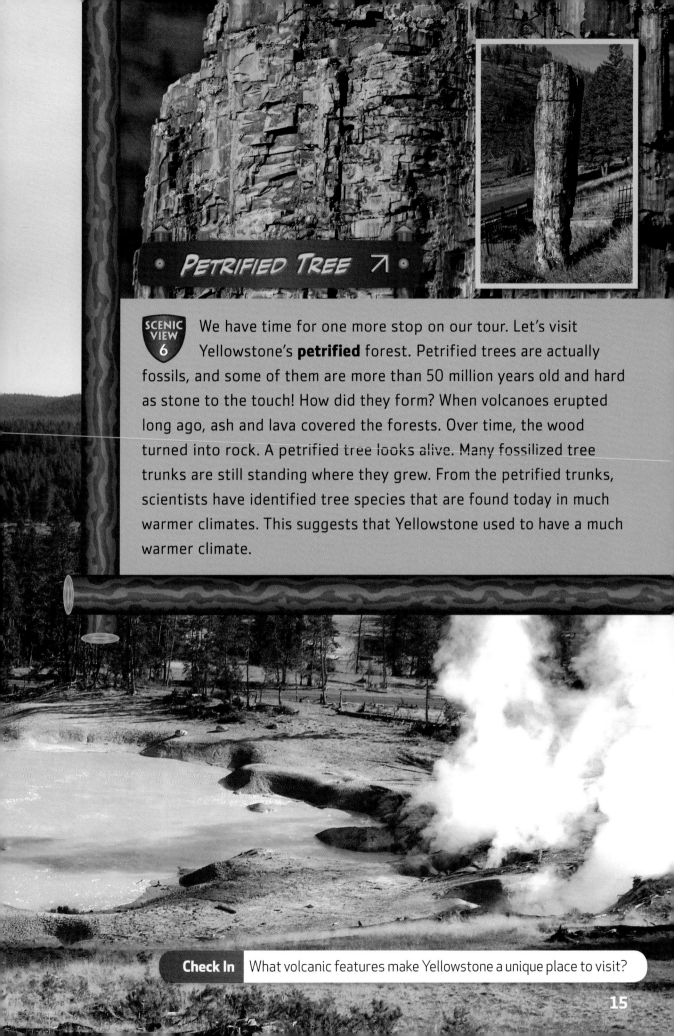

PETRIFIED TREE ↗

SCENIC VIEW 6 We have time for one more stop on our tour. Let's visit Yellowstone's **petrified** forest. Petrified trees are actually fossils, and some of them are more than 50 million years old and hard as stone to the touch! How did they form? When volcanoes erupted long ago, ash and lava covered the forests. Over time, the wood turned into rock. A petrified tree looks alive. Many fossilized tree trunks are still standing where they grew. From the petrified trunks, scientists have identified tree species that are found today in much warmer climates. This suggests that Yellowstone used to have a much warmer climate.

Check In What volcanic features make Yellowstone a unique place to visit?

YELLOWSTONE
TOO STRANGE TO BELIEVE

by Laura Mansilla | illustrated by Ron Borrensen

JOHN COLTER (1775–1813)

JOHN COLTER WAS AN EXPLORER. HE WAS A MEMBER OF THE LEWIS AND CLARK EXPEDITION THAT SET OUT TO SURVEY THE AMERICAN LANDSCAPE. ON THE RETURN JOURNEY, JOHN EXPLORED YELLOWSTONE. HE WAS PROBABLY THE FIRST PERSON OF EUROPEAN DESCENT TO SEE THE REGION.

JIM BRIDGER (1804–1881)

JIM BRIDGER WAS A TRAPPER, FUR TRADER, AND MOUNTAIN MAN. HE SET OUT TO EXPLORE THE YELLOWSTONE REGION IN THE LATE 1850S. JIM WAS WELL KNOWN DURING HIS LIFE AND AFTERWARD AS A GOOD STORYTELLER, ESPECIALLY A TELLER OF TALL TALES.

Mammoth Hot Springs ◉

Obsidian Cliff ◉   ◉ Petrified Tree

◉ Sizzling Basin Mud Pots

◉ Grand Prismatic
Spring

◉ Old Faithful
Geyser

THE FIRST EUROPEANS TO TRAVEL TO YELLOWSTONE WERE HUNTERS CALLED MOUNTAIN MEN. THEY WERE IN SEARCH OF BEAVERS, AS BEAVER FUR HATS WERE FASHIONABLE IN EUROPE AT THE TIME. WHEN THE MOUNTAIN MEN TRAVELED HOME, THEY TOLD ABOUT WHAT THEY HAD SEEN. BUT NO ONE BELIEVED THEIR STORIES, OR TALL TALES, AS THEY CALLED THEM.

JOHN COLTER WAS A MOUNTAIN MAN WHO PASSED THROUGH YELLOWSTONE. HE SAW AMAZING SIGHTS, SUCH AS GEYSERS SHOOTING WATER INTO THE AIR, HOT MUD BUBBLING FROM THE GROUND, AND CLOUDS OF SMELLY, SULFUROUS GASES.

COLTER TOLD THE PEOPLE HE MET ABOUT WHAT HE HAD SEEN. BUT NO ONE BELIEVED HIS WILD STORIES. COLTER DIDN'T CARE IF PEOPLE DIDN'T BELIEVE HIM. HE WAS MORE INTERESTED IN TRAPPING BEAVERS ANYWAY.

A FEW YEARS LATER, ANOTHER MOUNTAIN MAN NAMED JIM BRIDGER EXPLORED YELLOWSTONE. HE, TOO, MARVELED AT ALL THE NATURAL WONDERS THERE.

MANY OTHER MOUNTAIN MEN CAME THROUGH YELLOWSTONE. BUT BRIDGER WAS DIFFERENT. HE LIKED TO SPIN A YARN, WHICH MEANS HE LIKED TO TELL STORIES.

BRIDGER LOVED TO TELL STORIES ABOUT THE AMAZING THINGS HE HAD SEEN. HE LIKED TO EXAGGERATE, AND WITH EACH TELLING HE ADDED A LITTLE BIT MORE EXAGGERATION. IN TIME, FOLKS COULDN'T TELL WHAT WAS TRUE AND WHAT WASN'T.

ALL THE SAME, THOSE CITY FOLK LOVED TO HEAR ABOUT THE ADVENTURES OF THE MOUNTAIN MEN.

LET ME TELL YOU ABOUT THE FISHING IN YELLOWSTONE!

TELL US ABOUT THE HUNTING TOO!

IN YELLOWSTONE, THERE IS A SPRING OF BOILING WATER THAT FLOWS INTO A LAKE FULL OF BIG, FAT TROUT. THE HOT WATER FROM THE SPRING FLOATS ON TOP OF THE COLD LAKE WATER.

ALL YOU HAVE TO DO IS DIG UP SOME SPECIAL YELLOWSTONE WRIGGLING WORMS THAT WRIGGLE MORE THAN ANY OTHER WORMS IN THE WORLD. THEN YOU CAST YOUR FISHING LINE. ALL THAT WRIGGLING ATTRACTS THE TROUT THAT SWIM AROUND IN THE COLD LAKE WATER.

WHEN A TROUT BITES, YOU REEL IT IN, AND BY THE TIME THE FISH HAS BEEN PULLED THROUGH THE HOT WATER, IT'S COOKED AND READY TO EAT. THERE YOU HAVE IT: "INSTANT DINNER!"

19

JIM TOLD HUNTING STORIES, TOO. THERE WAS ONE TIME WHEN HE SPIED A LARGE ELK MUNCHING ON GRASS.

BANG!

HE REACHED A GOOD SHOOTING PLACE AND TOOK AIM.

JIM LOADED HIS GUN AND SNEAKED FORWARD. HE WAS GOOD AT SNEAKING, WHICH WAS A USEFUL SKILL IF YOU DEPENDED ON HUNTING FOR FOOD.

NOW, JIM WAS A GOOD SHOT, BUT TO HIS SURPRISE THE ANIMAL WAS STILL STANDING THERE MUNCHING GRASS. JIM SCRATCHED HIS HEAD, WONDERING HOW HE HAD MISSED SUCH AN EASY TARGET.

BANG!

HE RELOADED HIS GUN AND SNEAKED CLOSER.

JIM WAS NOW VERY CLOSE, AND HE RAISED HIS GUN AND TOOK EXTRA CAREFUL AIM.

JIM COULDN'T BELIEVE HIS EYES. HE HAD MISSED AGAIN! HE FIGURED HIS GUN WAS BENT OR HIS EYES WEREN'T SEEING RIGHT.

JIM RAN AT THE ELK, BUT HE HIT SOMETHING HARD THAT KNOCKED HIM BACKWARD.

HE THREW HIS GUN DOWN IN DISGUST, TOOK OUT HIS KNIFE, AND SNEAKED FORWARD AGAIN. STILL THE ELK DIDN'T HEAR HIM.

20

HE GOT UP, RUBBING HIS HEAD. WHAT HAD HE RUN INTO? JIM REACHED OUT HIS HAND AND FELT AROUND. HE HAD BUMPED INTO A WALL OF GLASS AS BIG AS A MOUNTAIN. NO WONDER HIS SHOTS HAD MISSED. THE ANIMAL WAS STANDING ON THE OTHER SIDE OF A GLASS MOUNTAIN.

JIM WENT TO BED HUNGRY THAT NIGHT.

RUMBLE
RUMBLE
RUMBLE

ONE DAY, JIM AND HIS HORSE WERE TRAVELING THROUGH YELLOWSTONE COUNTRY LOOKING FOR FOOD. IT HAD BEEN A DRY SUMMER, SO THE ANIMALS HAD ALL GONE IN SEARCH OF WATER. JIM WAS SO HUNGRY HE HAD EVEN EATEN ONE OF HIS MOCCASINS.

THEN, UP AHEAD, JIM SPIED A THICK, GREEN FOREST. THINKING HE WOULD FIND A MEAL THERE, HE RODE ON INTO THE TREES.

SURE ENOUGH, HE SAW RABBITS, SAGE HENS, AND BEARS. BUT THERE WAS SOMETHING VERY STRANGE ABOUT THE FOREST.

NOT ONE OF THE ANIMALS WAS MOVING, AND THE TREES WERE AS STILL AS STATUES. JIM TOOK OUT HIS HUNTING KNIFE AND SLASHED AT A TREE. SPARKS FLEW IN EVERY DIRECTION. HE TOOK A CLOSER LOOK AT THE TREE. "WHY, THIS TREE IS PETRIFIED!" JIM EXCLAIMED. PETRIFIED MEANS SOMETHING TURNED TO STONE.

JIM REALIZED THAT THE TREES, ANIMALS, AND EVEN THE GROUND WERE PETRIFIED. PETRIFIED BIRDS LOOKED AS IF THEY WERE FLYING, BUT THEY WERE AS STILL AS COULD BE.

JIM REALIZED THAT HE WASN'T GOING TO FIND DINNER IN A PETRIFIED FOREST. SO HE GOT BACK ON HIS HORSE AND RODE ON, CHEWING ON HIS OTHER MOCCASIN.

Check In How do these tall tales include actual features of Yellowstone's natural environment?

RETURN of the WOLF

by Lara Winegar

In the wilderness of Yellowstone you may hear a long, high-pitched howl. A shy animal that many people fear makes this sound. The gray wolf has been written about for years, and it is now the subject of heated debates.

The gray wolf is native to North America. But as people settled in the United States during the 1800s, they didn't want **predatory** animals near them. People thought wolves were a threat to cattle and sheep. So people were paid to kill wolves. By the 1930s, wolves were nearly extinct in most of the United States.

In 1995, the gray wolf was brought back to Yellowstone. Some people supported this decision. Others did not.

As long as people have lived near wolves, they have had opinions about them. An opinion is a person's point of view or a judgment. Opinions are not always based on facts. The return of the wolf has affected people who live near the park. Some people think wolves are vicious predators. Others see wolves as an important part of the Yellowstone ecosystem, or all the plants, animals, and nonliving things in the park's environment. Analyze the opinions that follow. Then decide which you are more likely to agree with.

A Rancher's Opinion

Ranches are large farms where livestock such as cattle and sheep are raised for food. Ranching is essential to the economy in the Yellowstone area. Loss of livestock can cause financial trouble for ranchers.

In the last few centuries, people traveled west to create better lives for their families. Settlers needed a way to earn a living. Ranching became a way to use the land to make money.

In the early 20th century, people were paid to kill wolves. This payment is called a bounty. Wolves were seen as predators and as a threat to livestock. Ranchers knew they would lose money if the wolves harmed their livestock, so many ranchers accepted these bounties.

Wolves were brought back to Yellowstone in 1995. Their numbers have grown ever since. Wolves travel over large ranges and often end up on ranches. Sometimes wolves kill and eat cattle or sheep. By law, ranchers cannot kill a wolf unless they see it attacking their livestock. Ranchers are frustrated and concerned. They are unable to protect their livestock.

Wolves are predatory animals. Many ranchers believe that wolves do not belong in the park. They think they will lose money if wolves kill their livestock. So many ranchers want the wolves removed permanently.

A Conservationist's Opinion

Conservationists have a different opinion than ranchers about bringing wolves back to Yellowstone. Conservationists want to protect natural habitats. They also believe that areas changed by humans should be restored to nature.

Wolves have lived in the area for thousands of years. Long before ranchers came to the area, wolves were part of Yellowstone.

Conservationists believe that wolves were only removed from Yellowstone because people were paid a bounty to kill them. Since wolves are an **indigenous**, or native, species, they should be brought back to Yellowstone.

Conservationists also argue that wolves are important to the health of the environment. Wolves play an important role in the ecosystem.

As predators, wolves control the number of **prey** animals such as elk and bison. Without wolves, there would be too many prey animals in Yellowstone. Too many prey animals would eventually harm the ecosystem.

Wolves do kill livestock. However, conservationists believe wolves rarely kill cattle and sheep because there is plenty of natural prey in Yellowstone. Conservationists believe that it was a good decision to reintroduce wolves to Yellowstone.

A Scientist's Opinion

For years, scientists discussed bringing the gray wolf back to Yellowstone. Before people removed them, wolves were among the top-level predators of the **food web**, or all the food chains in an ecosystem. Now that wolves are back, they can be studied using scientific methods. Scientists want to know how the gray wolf affects the ecosystem. Scientists put their own opinions aside. They gather information in a neutral way.

When the wolves were first released in 1995, they wore tracking collars. These collars helped scientists track where the wolves traveled, what they ate, and how long they lived.

Wolves affect other species in Yellowstone. For example, elk are always on the lookout for wolves.

Instead of grazing in one place for too long, elk move from place to place. This stops the elk from overeating certain trees. Now that the trees are able to grow again, beavers are using those trees for food and shelter. As a result, the number of beavers has grown.

Scientists spent a lot of time developing a plan before they brought the wolves back to Yellowstone. Wolves that attack livestock or get too used to people are removed. Safety for people, and for the wolves, is important.

You may develop your own opinion about the wolves in Yellowstone. However, these animals are giving scientists a chance to study a top predator. Scientists can use this information to help make decisions in the future.

▽ Scientists sometimes tranquilize the wolves so they can examine them closely.

Check In | Whose point of view do you most agree with? Why?

Discuss

1. What connections can you make among the four selections in *Yellowstone National Park?* How do you think the selections are related?

2. Engraved on the Roosevelt Arch is the phrase, "For the Benefit and Enjoyment of the People." Do you think this phrase might be true for all national parks? Why?

3. Compare the tall tales with the volcanic tour of Yellowstone. How are Jim Bridger's tall tale descriptions similar to the real thing? In what ways are the tales exaggerated?

4. What are some of the effects of wolf reintroduction on the environment and the people who live near Yellowstone? What is your opinion about the situation?

5. What do you still wonder about the environment in Yellowstone and the issues that surround it?